## Gail Lawther's QUICK QUILTS

GW00750256

# Doodlebugs

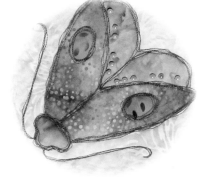

## Contents

## TEAMWORK CRAFTBOOKS

# Introduction

Quilting for me is all about enjoyment and creativity, and in recent years I've been having lots of fun creating fused designs that are really quick and easy to assemble. I designed a whole collection of them for our book *Stained Glass Patchwork Techniques: BIRDS*, and they proved so popular that I kept coming up with more ideas.

So, here is another collection – this time featuring bugs instead of birds! These cute dragonflies, butterflies, moths, beetles and bees make great wall-hangings, mini-quilts and cushion-covers; there are all kinds of ways you can combine and vary the designs, depending on the colours you use, the number of squares you create, and the way you add borders and sashing.

The motifs also work well for smaller projects: Kindle ™ cover, glasses case, needle-case, cards, bags etc. And you can add even more variation by embellishing the designs with hand or machine embroidery and/or beads and charms. The examples on the left show just how different the same basic motif can look, depending on the fabric choices and the ways in which you embellish the patches.

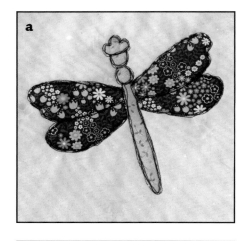

a

We modern-day stitchers have all kinds of wonderful things available to us, and one of the very best is: double-sided bonding web. All the designs in this booklet are created by fusing the motifs onto the background with bonding web, then many of them use my 'scribble-quilting' technique (**a**) to produce a subtle stained-glass effect round the patches. If you prefer, though, you could use blanket stitch (**b**) – hand or machine – or satin stitch (**c**) around the patches for a different effect. If you fancy either of these last two ideas, you could also enlarge the templates a little and put the designs on larger squares; the increased size of the patches will make them easier to stitch around. The important thing is to have fun – and to create designs that you and your loved ones will enjoy.

**So, welcome to *Doodlebugs!***

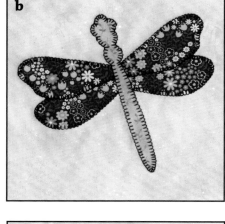

b

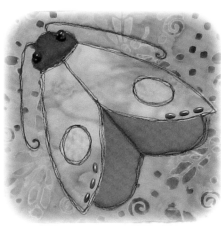

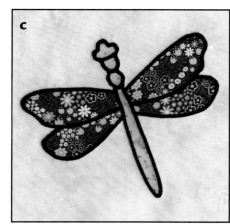

c

## Working with bonding web

There are various types available, but they all work in a similar way, allowing you to bond one piece of fabric to another pretty permanently. The ones I like best are Bondaweb ™ and Steam-a-Seam ™; Steam-a-Seam has the extra benefit that you can finger-press the patches in position before you fuse them permanently. Of course we are stitchers, not gluers, and all these projects are also quilted; on page 4 you'll find details of how to do my 'scribble-quilting', or doodling, technique.

The basic method for working with bonding web follows these steps:

1   Using ordinary pencil, and working on the smooth (non-glue) side of the bonding web, trace your chosen shape (**a**).

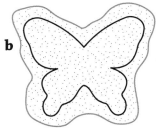

2   Cut the shape out roughly, leaving a margin of bonding web outside the drawn line (**b**); this helps you to get a really good seal when you fuse the shape onto the fabric.

3   Position the paper shape, glue side down, on the back of your chosen fabric (**c**); make sure that the fabric patch is slightly larger all round than the bonding web shape. (This

will help you keep your ironing board free of sticky areas!)

4   Lay a greaseproof/non-stick sheet over the work, and use a hot iron to fuse the shape firmly to the fabric. The bonding web manufacturers differ on whether they suggest steam or not; I've found that it doesn't seem to make too much difference.

5   Cut the shape out along the marked line (**d**). This is where the small, sharp scissors come into play; make sure that yours are really sharp right to the tips, so that you're creating a good, crisp edge.

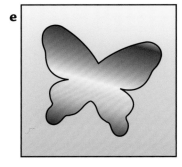

6   Once you're ready to fuse the shape into position on another fabric, peel off the backing paper. Position the shape, glue side down, on the right side of the background fabric (**e**); cover with the greaseproof/non-stick sheet, and iron the patch in place until it's firmly fused.

## Tips for working with bonding web

❋ When you can, use tightly-woven fabrics such as batiks; these will help you to keep really sharp outlines on the patches. Polyester/cotton sheeting also works well, as it too has a very close weave.

❋ Always use a non-stick ironing sheet (or a piece of greaseproof paper/baking parchment) to protect the iron and board from stray stickiness; it's worth doing this even when you're fusing the patches onto the background fabrics. You can buy non-stick ironing sheets very cheaply in pound shops ...

❋ Remember that the bonding web always goes on the back of the fabric, glue (rough) side of the bonding web against the wrong side of the fabric.

❋ Steam-a-Seam has paper on both sides of the glue web to protect it, as it's quite sticky. When you've traced shapes onto one side, and want to peel off the backing paper, make sure that the glue web stays attached to the traced side!

❋ Use a good hot iron to fuse on the bonding web (the hottest suitable for the fabrics you're working with); this will help to ensure a really good bond between the layers. If you're using Bondaweb, the paper will go translucent instead of white, which shows that the glue has stuck well.

❋ When you come to remove the backing papers from the fused shapes, scratch the paper with a pin; this breaks the static seal and makes it much easier to peel the paper off.

## Scribble-quilting/doodling

My scribbling/doodling technique combines fusing with free machine quilting, working in dark thread to create a subtle stained glass effect. If you're new to free machine quilting, this is the perfect place to start, because (to be quite honest) it doesn't really matter where the lines go! The trick is to work several random lines of free machining round the edge of each shape, allowing each stitching line to meander between the appliqué patch and the background. It's as easy as doodling.

To do this technique, you need to set your sewing machine up for free quilting. Machines vary enormously in exactly how this is done – consult your manual for the details – but generally you need to do two things: attach a free machining foot (which is usually an open or closed ring of metal or plastic); and drop or cover the feed dogs – the little teeth that normally pull the fabric under the machine foot evenly. You can then move the fabric in any direction, which allows you to follow the shapes of the motifs really easily.

Once your motif is fused onto the background, and you've layered up your quilt with the wadding and backing (**a**), choose a place to begin stitching. Before you start, bring the bobbin thread up to the surface of the work, so that it won't get tangled up at the back. Begin with lines that, visually, go into/under other lines – so, on the little Blue Peter sequence below, I'm beginning with the beetle's under-body, working three or more lines of stitching flowing freely round the edges of the shape (**b**).

Carry on building up the design in the same way until all the raw edges are covered and you've added any internal lines and details such as antennae (**c** and **d**). If you want a stronger effect from the stitching, use four or five lines.

## Before you begin ...

I've done six basic designs using the collection of bug motifs, and on the following pages I'll show you how to put them together, but you will think of lots of other ways of combining and embellishing the motifs. And, of course, you can also enlarge the shapes and use them on all kinds of other items; larger versions edged with satin stitch or blanket stitch would make great motifs for bags to hold kids' books, shoes or toys.

### Whichever design you're doing, you will need:

- machine-quilting thread in a dark colour that contrasts well with your chosen fabrics (eg black, navy, dark green, dark purple, dark brown)
- sewing thread to match any borders, binding, sashing or cushion backings
- pencil
- non-stick ironing sheet or greaseproof paper/baking parchment; use this to protect the iron and ironing board whenever you're working with the bonding web
- small, sharp-pointed scissors – these are important: if yours aren't sharp right to the tip, now's the time to invest in some new ones!
- Frixion ™ pen or chalk marker (for drawing on any extra details you want to quilt, such as antennae)
- pad of small Post-It ™ notes, or scraps of paper and pins (for numbering your background squares so that you can keep them in the right order)
- rotary cutter, ruler and board
- optional embellishments: beads, charms, jewels, buttons etc

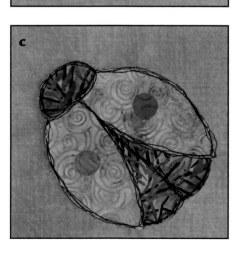

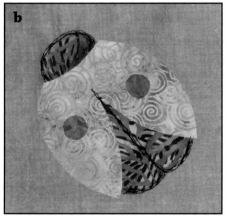

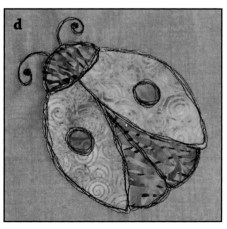

# Nine-Bug Panel

Let's begin with a showcase for all the main motifs: your very own bug collection! As I explain in the instructions, you can mix and match the various shapes – for instance, the templates include four different basic butterfly outlines and four different dragonfly wing shapes etc, along with other motifs (hearts, circles, ovals) you can use to decorate many of the bugs. If you are using very decorative fabrics – for instance, strong prints or vividly-patterned batiks – you may want to keep the basic shapes quite simple

and unadorned. And don't forget, too, that you can add all kinds of hand and machine embroidery, buttons, beads, charms etc to personalise the final quilt.

*Finished size roughly 20in (51cm) square*

## As well as the items on page 4, you will also need:

❀ nine 6in (15cm) background squares of cotton fabric; these can all be different, or you can use two or three fabrics that complement each other

- large scraps of cotton fabrics in a mixture of colours and tones that work well against your background squares
- border; two 18 x 2in (46 x 5cm) strips, two 20 x 2in (51 x 5cm) strips
- backing fabric, 22in (56cm) square
- 2¼yd (2.1m) binding strip (I used a single binding cut 1¾in/4.5cm wide); this can either be the same as the border fabric, or a contrast
- 1yd (1m) double-sided bonding web, 18in (46cm) wide, or the equivalent in smaller pieces
- flat wadding, 22in (56cm) square

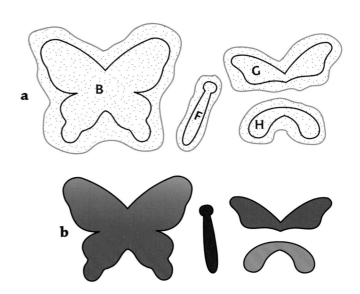

## Instructions

1  Choose nine background squares and lay them out in the order they'll appear; write the numbers 1-9 on Post-It notes or scraps of paper, and stick/pin these to the squares in order. (This way, you'll remember which one goes where if they get mixed up during the stitching.) Now, working with the templates on pages 21-24, choose the bugs that you would like to feature on your design, and which one you want on which background square.

2  Use pencil to trace the chosen shapes – including the body shapes, if you're doing butterflies or dragonflies – onto the smooth side of the bonding web; leave a small gap between all the shapes, and write the relevant letter on each one to remind you what's what. Finally, choose the shapes that you'd like to use to decorate each bug; for instance, you can use pieces G and H on any of the butterfly designs, or you could use one of the circle, oval or heart shapes (N, X and Y) instead of one or both patches. Similarly, you can decorate the beetles with their matching wing patches, or with any of the extra decorative shapes. Once you've chosen, trace all these shapes in the same way onto the bonding web, adding the letters as before.

3  Cut all the shapes out roughly, leaving a border of bonding web around the pencil lines (a). Lay each bonding web piece, glue side down, onto the wrong side of the relevant fabric and fuse it in place with a warm iron; always use the non-stick or protective sheet between the work and the iron when you're fusing. Once everything is fused in place, carefully cut out all the motifs along the marked pencil lines (b).

4  Peel the papers off the main shapes; with each one, scratch the paper with a pin – this makes it much easier to peel the paper off. Lay each shape right side up on the right side of the relevant background square, and pin them roughly in place; now remove the papers from the bodies/wings/details and pin them in position. Make sure that all the patches are at least ½in (roughly 1cm) in from the outer edge, to allow room for the seams. Once you're happy with the arrangements, fuse the shapes in position (c).

5  Using ¼in seams throughout, join the squares first of all into rows, and then join the rows to create the centre of the design (d). Make sure as you join each row that the squares are the correct way up!

I found that it worked better to do the machine quilting before I added the borders; this way, the borders neatened out any unevenness in the final edge of the pieced design.

**6** Lay the backing fabric right side down on a flat surface and position the wadding on top; lay the fused design, right side up, on top so that there's an even border of wadding all the way around the edge of the design. Use your preferred method to secure the layers. If you've included a bee in your design and want to stitch the veins on the wings, draw them in with Frixion pen or chalk marker at this stage; do the same with any antennae etc. Follow the principles on page 4 to 'doodle' round the edges of the shapes (**e**), beginning with any lines that go into other lines – eg, stitch the veins on the bee's wings before you outline them, and stitch the edges of each butterfly's wings before you do its body. Use ¼in seams to add the shorter borders to the sides of the design; trim the borders to fit if necessary, then add and trim the top and bottom borders in the same way (**f**).

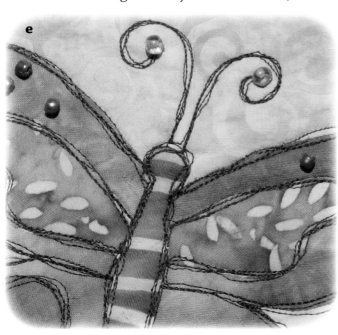

**7** Use a rotary cutter, ruler and board to trim the quilt down to an accurate square, and use the binding strip to add a continuous binding around the raw edges. Add any embellishments (buttons, beads, charms etc) you wish. To hang the quilt, add a hidden casing at the top of the quilt on the back, or stitch on hanging loops of ribbon or tape.

*The quilts below show just how much you can vary nine-bug panels. Try playing around with different colours and fabric styles; pick a different selection of bugs, and vary the colour of thread you use for the 'doodling'*

# Bright Bugs

This quilt has a bit of a Jacobean feel, created by the basic black-and-white colourscheme enhanced with bright accents; I've also embellished the designs with decorative machine embroidery. If you want to use this kind of dense machine embroidery, work with a tear-away backing such as Stitch 'n' Tear ™ behind the work. This will help you produce a really even piece of embroidery, but stops the close stitching from distorting the work.

*Finished size roughly 8 x 28in (20 x 71cm)*

## As well as the items on page 4, you will also need:

❀ four 6in (15cm) background squares of cotton fabric; these can all be the same, or you can use several fabrics that complement each other (I used four different black-and-white prints)

❀ large scraps of cotton fabrics in a mixture of colours and tones that work well against your background squares (I used colours to echo my border fabrics)

❀ borders; four 6in (15cm) squares of cotton fabric that contrast with your background squares (I used four different bright colours)

❀ backing fabric, 10 x 30in (25 x 75cm)

❀ double-sided bonding web, 15in (38cm) square, or the equivalent in smaller pieces

❀ flat wadding, 10 x 30in (25 x 75cm)

❀ tearaway foundation paper (eg Stitch 'n' Tear) if you're adding any machine satin-stitch or similar

## Instructions

**1** Lay the four background squares out in the order they'll appear; write the numbers 1-4 on Post-It notes or scraps of paper, and stick/pin these to the squares in order. (This way, you'll remember which one goes where if they get mixed up during the stitching.) Now choose the bugs that you would like to feature on your design, and which one you want on which background square. Use pencil to trace the chosen shapes onto the smooth side of the bonding web; leave a small gap between all the shapes, and write the relevant number on each one. Finally, choose the shapes that you'd like to use to decorate each bug. Once you've chosen, trace these and any relevant body or extra wing shapes in the same way, numbering them as before.

**2** Cut all the shapes out roughly, leaving a border of bonding web around the pencil lines. Lay each bonding web piece, glue side down, onto the wrong side of the relevant fabric and fuse it in place with a warm iron; once everything is fused in place, carefully cut out all the designs along the marked pencil lines.

**3** Peel the papers off the main shapes; with each one, scratch the paper with a pin – this makes it much easier to peel the paper off. Lay each shape right side up on the relevant background square, and pin them roughly in place; now remove the papers from the bodies/wings/details and pin them in position. Make sure that all the patches are at least ½in (roughly 1cm) in from the outer edge, to allow room for the seams. Once you're happy with the arrangements, fuse all the shapes in position on the background squares (**a**).

**4** Use the rotary cutter, ruler and board to cut the four background squares as shown (**b**); you will then have four long triangular shapes in each fabric. Lay one of these shapes on the relevant bug square, right sides together, and matching the corners of

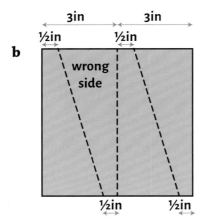

the shapes as shown (**c**); stitch a ¼in seam, leaving this first seam open for ½in (1.5cm) at the lower end. Press the seam to the darker side, then add the second border piece in the same way (**d**); you don't need to leave this seam open.

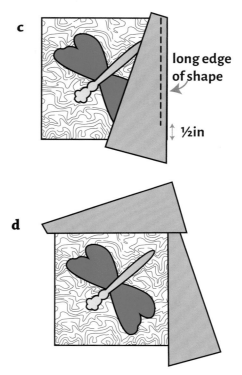

**5** Add the other two border pieces, then complete the first seam to finish the block (**e**). Use the rotary cutter, ruler and board to trim each block down to an accurate square; they should each measure 7½in square, but that's not crucial as long as they're all the same size.

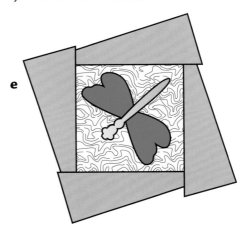

**6** Using ¼in seams, join the squares into a long rectangle (**f**). Lay the backing fabric right side down on a flat surface and position the wadding on top; lay the fused design, right side up, on top so that there's an even border of wadding all the way around the edge of the design. Use your preferred method to secure the layers. If you wish, embellish some of the patches with lines of decorative machine embroidery. If you're using a pattern that is quite dense, position a bit of tearaway foundation fabric behind the work before you stitch, then tear it away afterwards – this will give you a better, smoother surface and prevent the embroidery from distorting the surface.

If you've included a bee in your design and want to stitch the veins on the wings, draw them in with Frixion pen or chalk marker at this stage; do the same with any antennae etc. Follow the tips on page 4 to 'doodle' round these lines and the edges of the fused shapes (**g**).

**f**

**g**

**7** Use a rotary cutter, ruler and board to trim the quilt down to an accurate rectangle, and use the binding strip to add a continuous binding around the raw edges. Add any embellishments (buttons, beads, charms etc) you wish. To hang the quilt, add a hidden casing at the top of the quilt on the back, or stitch on hanging loops of ribbon or tape.

*All kinds of colours will work for the decorative stitching; in the example below, which I've called* Tutankhamen's Beetles, *I've used gold and turquoise.*

# Lovebug Cushion-Cover

Bright folksy prints are great fun to work with, and I've used them with my bug designs to create a cheery cushion-cover. To pick up the Lovebug theme, I hunted out heart-shaped beads and buttons in various colours to complement the fabrics. You could also create variations of my Lovebugs in neutral colours, perhaps using a variety of ethnic-print fabrics embellished with wooden heart buttons – or a very modern bright design decorated with metallic hearts; for more ideas, see the examples on page 13.

*Finished size roughly 18in (46cm) square*

**As well as the items on page 4, you will also need:**

❀ four 6in (15cm) background squares of pale-to-medium cotton fabric; these can all be the same, or you can use several fabrics that complement each other

❀ large scraps of cotton fabrics in a mixture of colours and tones that work well against your background squares (I used bright, folksy prints)

- inner borders; four 6in (15cm) squares of cotton fabric that contrast with your background squares
- outer border; two 15 x 2½in (38 x 6.5cm) strips, two 20 x 2½in (51 x 6.5cm) strips
- backing fabric (eg calico), 21in (53cm) square
- fabric for the back of the cushion-cover, two 12 x 19in (30 x 49cm) rectangles
- double-sided bonding web, 15in (38cm) square, or the equivalent in smaller pieces
- flat wadding, 21in (53cm) square

## Instructions

1  Follow steps 1-4 for the *Bright Bugs* (see pages 8-9) to create the four bug squares, but when you are cutting the borders, cut two of the border squares one way (**a**), and the other two with the angles reversed (**b**). Once the borders are added, you will then have two blocks angled one way and two the other way (**c**).

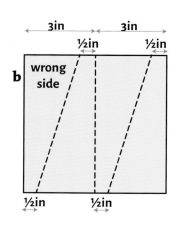

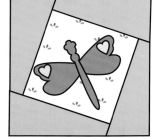

2  Using ¼in seams, join the blocks first of all into rows and then into a square (**d**). Use ¼in seams to add the shorter borders to the top and bottom of the design; trim the borders to fit the raw edges, then add the side borders in the same way (**e**).

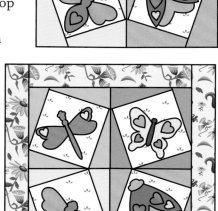

3  Lay the backing fabric right side down on a flat surface, and lay the wadding and then the fused design, right side up, on top so that there's an even border of wadding all the way around the edge of the design. Use your preferred method to secure the layers. If you've included a bee in your design and want to stitch veins on the wings, or to add any antennae on the bugs, draw them in with Frixion pen or chalk marker at this stage. Follow the tips on page 4 to 'doodle' round these lines and the edges of the fused shapes (**f**).

**4** Use a rotary cutter, ruler and board to trim the quilt down to an accurate square. Fold under and stitch a small double seam on one long edge of each backing rectangle (**g**). Lay the quilted square right side up on a flat surface, and position the two backing pieces on top, right sides down, overlapping them so that all the raw edges align. Pin, then stitch a ¼-½in seam all the way around the edge of the square (**h**); clip the corners, turn out, and press the edges of the cushion-cover. Add any embellishments (buttons, beads, charms etc) you wish to complete the design.

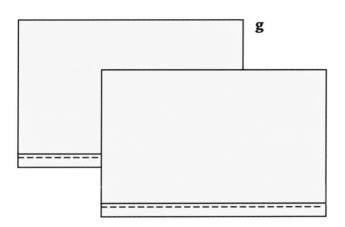

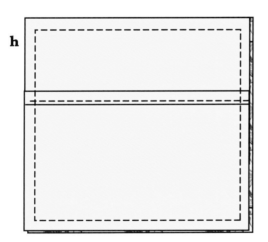

*In the examples on the right, I've created three different variations of the* Lovebugs. *The top version is made in toning green-and-white prints, and simply decorated with heart-shaped glass beads. In the centre version I managed to find various sumptuous red, gold and cream heart-print fabrics, and also added gold fabric hearts embellished with red heart buttons.*

*The bottom version has an ethnic, homespun feel with brown-and-beige prints and some tiny heart-shaped buttons; this version would also look good decorated with wooden buttons and/or beads.*

# Illuminated Bugs

I love illuminated manuscripts – I actually asked for a facsimile of the *Duc de Berry's Book of Hours* as my 21st birthday present. I can't get enough of the jewel-bright colours and sumptuous decoration. Often in these manuscripts you find gorgeous plants embellishing the margins, sometimes accompanied by equally exquisite butterflies or beetles, and in this little panel I've stitched my own illuminated bugs. You can have great fun embellishing this design with all kinds of glitzy beads, charms and fake gems.

*Finished size 16in (41cm) square*

## As well as the items on page 4, you will also need:

- four 6in (15cm) background squares of cotton fabric; these can all be the same, or you can use several fabrics that complement each other (I used four different gold-and-cream prints)

- large scraps of cotton fabrics in a mixture of colours and tones that work well against your background squares (I used bright, exotic prints and dark golds)

- ❈ border and sashings; two 6 x 2in (15 x 5cm) strips, three 13 x 2in (33 x 5cm) strips, two 16 x 2in (41 x 5cm) strips
- ❈ backing fabric, 18in (46cm) square
- ❈ double-sided bonding web, 15in (38cm) square, or the equivalent in smaller pieces
- ❈ flat wadding, 18in (46cm) square
- ❈ 2yd (2m) binding strip (I used a single binding cut 2¼in/6cm wide); this can either be the same as the border fabric, or a contrast

## Instructions

1 Follow steps 1-3 for the *Bright Bugs* (see pages 8-9) to create four bug squares (**a**). Using ¼in seams, add one short strip of sashing between squares 1 and 3, and the other between squares 2 and 4 (**b**).

**a**

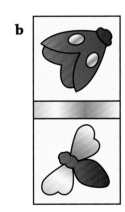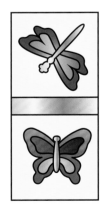

**b**

2 Next, add the three middle-length sashing/border strips to the sides and between the rows as shown (**c**). Finally, add the two long strips to the top and bottom to create the quilt top (**d**).

**c**

**d**

3 Lay the backing fabric right side down on a flat surface and position the wadding on top; lay the fused design, right side up, on top so that there's an even border of wadding all the way around the edge of the design. Use your preferred method to secure the layers. If you've included a bee in your design and want to stitch the veins on the wings, draw them in with Frixion pen or chalk marker at this stage; do the same with any antennae etc. Follow the tips on page 4 to 'doodle' round the edges of the fused shapes (**e**).

**e**

4 Use a rotary cutter, ruler and board to trim the quilt down to an accurate square, and use the binding strip to add a continuous binding around the raw edges. Embellish the designs as much as you like with fake gems and jewels, to add to the illuminated effect. To hang the quilt, add a hidden casing at the top of the quilt on the back, or stitch on hanging loops of ribbon or tape.

# Busy Bees

I loved the idea of doing some of the bee shapes within hexagons, to echo the cells of their honeycomb, and this little wall-hanging was the result. As I'd used a bright dotty print for the wings, I didn't feel that they needed stitched veins; similarly, I chose a bright print in funky stripes for the bodies, which again meant that they didn't need extra stripes. The patches are edged in machine satin stitch; I chose bright colours that complemented the cheery fabric prints. Of course you can use as many hexagons as you fancy, to create a larger hanging – whatever you do, it will look the bee's knees!

*Finished size roughly 8 x 21in (20 x 53cm)*

## As well as the items on page 4, you will also need:

- three 8 x 9in (20 x 23cm) pieces of cotton background fabric; these can all be the same, or you can use three different fabrics that complement each other (I used a simple blue-and-white print)
- three 9 x 11in (23 x 28 cm) rectangles of cotton fabric for backing/binding each panel; choose three different colours that echo the patches you're using for the bees, or make them all the same
- bright print fabrics for the wings (7in/18cm square), and the bodies (6in/15cm square), and six small beads for the eyes
- double-sided bonding web, 15in (38cm) square, or the equivalent in smaller pieces
- three 9in (23cm) squares of flat wadding
- bright threads for the satin stitch
- three 7in (18cm) squares of tearaway foundation fabric, such as Stitch 'n' Tear
- tracing or photocopy of the hexagon template on page 18

## Instructions

1 Cut out the hexagon template and use it as a pattern to cut hexagons from the three squares of background fabric. On the paper side of the bonding web, trace three bee wing shapes (template O), and three bee body shapes (template P) and cut the shapes out in groups, leaving a margin of bonding web around the edges – if you want to use particular sections of the fabric patterns, cut each paper shape out separately.

**2** Fuse the bonding web shapes onto the wrong sides of the appropriate fabrics and cut them out (**a**).

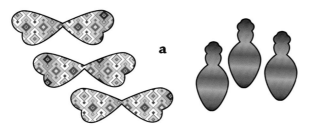

Peel off the papers, and position one wing patch on each background hexagon with a body shape on top; I found it more interesting to vary the directions of the bees on the hexagons (**b**). Make sure that the patches are at least ½in away from each of the raw edges, and once you're happy with their positions, fuse them in place.

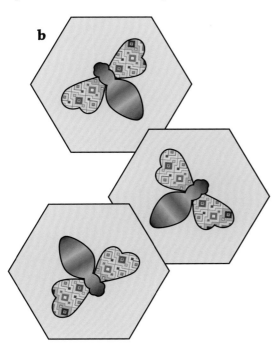

binding square and use the rotary cutter/ruler/board to cut a shape 1in larger all round than the paper hexagon – do the same with the other two pieces (**d**).

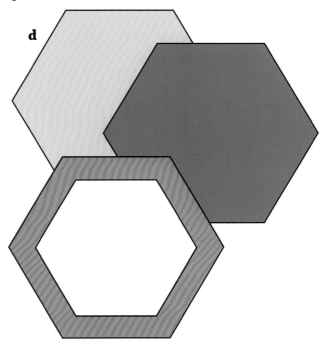

**3** Lay the squares of tearaway foundation paper on a flat surface and cover each one with a square of wadding; position one bee design on each, and pin the layers together. Set your machine up for satin stitch (basically, a zigzag stitch worked so closely that there are no gaps), and decide what width you'd like – I used a width of about 4. On each bee, work satin stitch round the lower wings, then the upper wings, and finally the body (**c**), varying the colours if you wish.

**4** At the back of the work, tear away the excess paper from around each bee shape. Use a rotary cutter, ruler and board to trim each piece of wadding down to the size of the background hexagon. Now pin the hexagon template onto one backing/

**5** Lay each backing shape right side down on a flat surface and position a bee design, right side up, on top so that there's an even border of fabric all the way around (**e**).

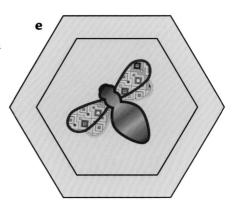

Fold the excess fabric to the front in a double fold to create an even border, and stitch the folded edge down by hand or machine (**f**).

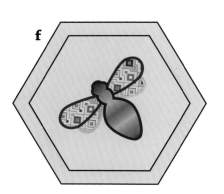

**f**

**6** Decide on the order you'd like for the hexagons, and position the first two right sides together. Using a neutral-coloured thread, oversew the two edges together at the join – make sure that you're joining the correct edges! Add the third hexagon in the same way. To hang the quilt, add a little casing on the back, or hanging loops of ribbon or tape, or simply stitch on a couple of curtain rings.

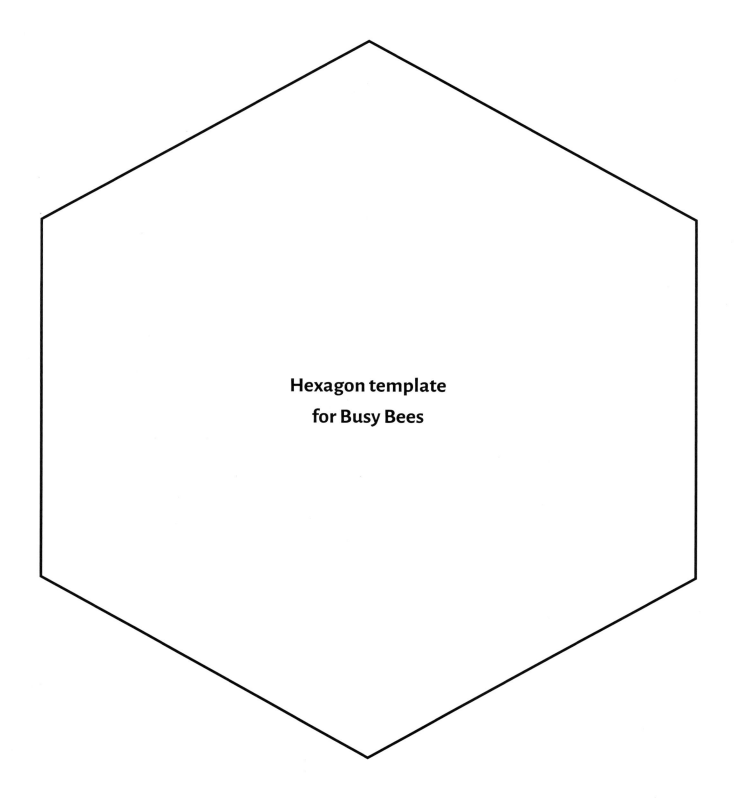

**Hexagon template**
**for Busy Bees**

# Playmat/Cot Quilt

Our finale for this booklet is this lovely design, which any baby or toddler would love – or you could stitch it in batiks for a more 'grown-up' quilt! On this project I wanted to edge the patches with machine blanket stitch, so I enlarged my chosen templates by 141% (A4 to A3 on the photocopier). Instead of adding any small decorative details on the bugs, I used a bright striped fabric on each design, and picked the other fabrics to complement the stripe – then a dark blue for the blanket stitch.

*Finished size roughly 33in (84cm) square*

### As well as the items on page 4, you will also need:

- ❀ nine 9in (23cm) background squares of cotton fabric; these can all be the same, or you can use several fabrics that complement each other
- ❀ large scraps of cotton fabrics in a mixture of colours and tones that work well against your background squares

- border and sashings; six 9 x 2½in (23 x 6.5cm) strips, four 30 x 2½in (76 x 6.5cm) strips, two 35 x 2½in (90 x 6.5cm) strips
- backing fabric, 35in (90cm) square
- double-sided bonding web, 30 x 18in (76 x 46cm), or the equivalent in smaller pieces
- flat wadding, 35in (90cm) square
- 4yd (4m) binding strip (I used a single binding cut 2¼in/6cm wide)
- enlarged versions of your chosen templates

## Instructions

1 Follow steps 1-4 for the Nine-Bug Panel (see page 6) to assemble nine squares decorated with fused bug designs. Using ¼in seams, add short strips of sashing between squares 1, 2 and 3 to create a row; do the same with the other two rows (**a**).

2 Next, add the four middle-length sashing/border strips to the top and bottom and between the rows as shown (**b**). Finally, add the two long strips to the sides to create the quilt top (**c**).

3 Lay the backing fabric right side down on a flat surface and position the wadding on top; lay the fused design, right side up, on top so that there's an even border of wadding all the way around the edge of the design. Use your preferred method to secure the layers. Set your machine up for blanket stitch, and try the stitch out on some scrap fabric, adjusting the width and length until you achieve the effect you're looking for.

4 Begin in the centre of the quilt, and on each bug start stitching on any lines that go into other lines – for instance, outline the edges of each butterfly's wings before you do its body. Continue in the same way with each bug until all the edges of the motifs are outlined. Once you've done all the blanket stitch, use any other machine stitches you fancy to create antennae etc (**d**) – or embroider these by hand.

5 Use a rotary cutter, ruler and board to trim the quilt down to an accurate square, and use the binding strip to add a continuous binding around the raw edges.

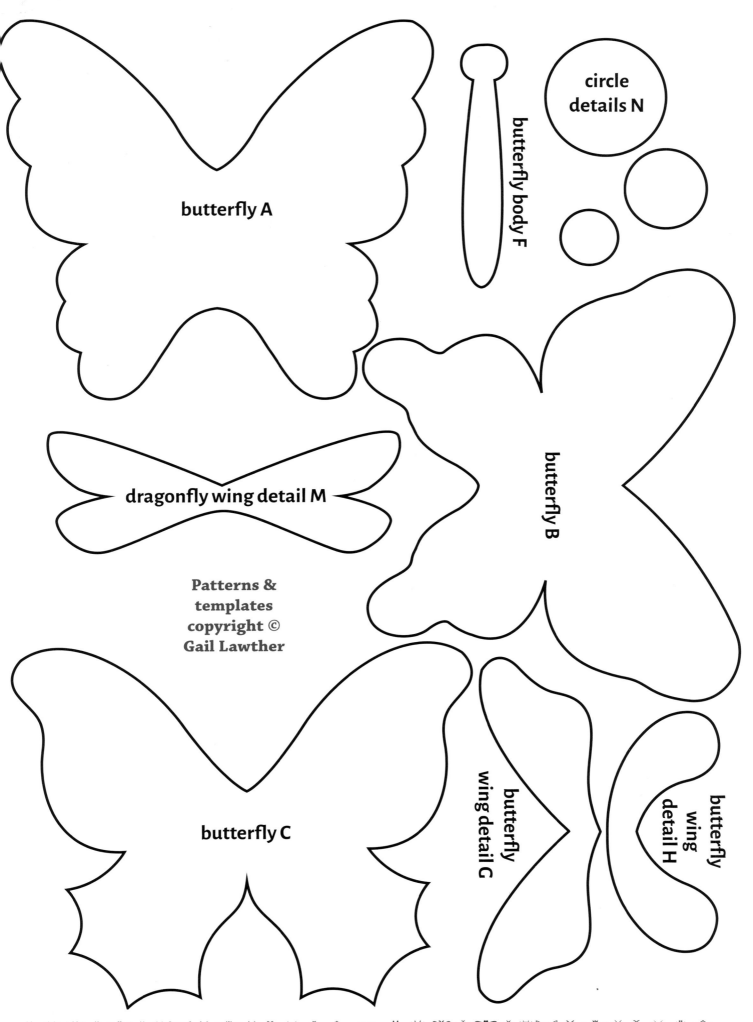

butterfly A

butterfly body F

circle
details N

dragonfly wing detail M

butterfly B

Patterns &
templates
copyright ©
Gail Lawther

butterfly C

butterfly
wing detail G

butterfly
wing
detail H

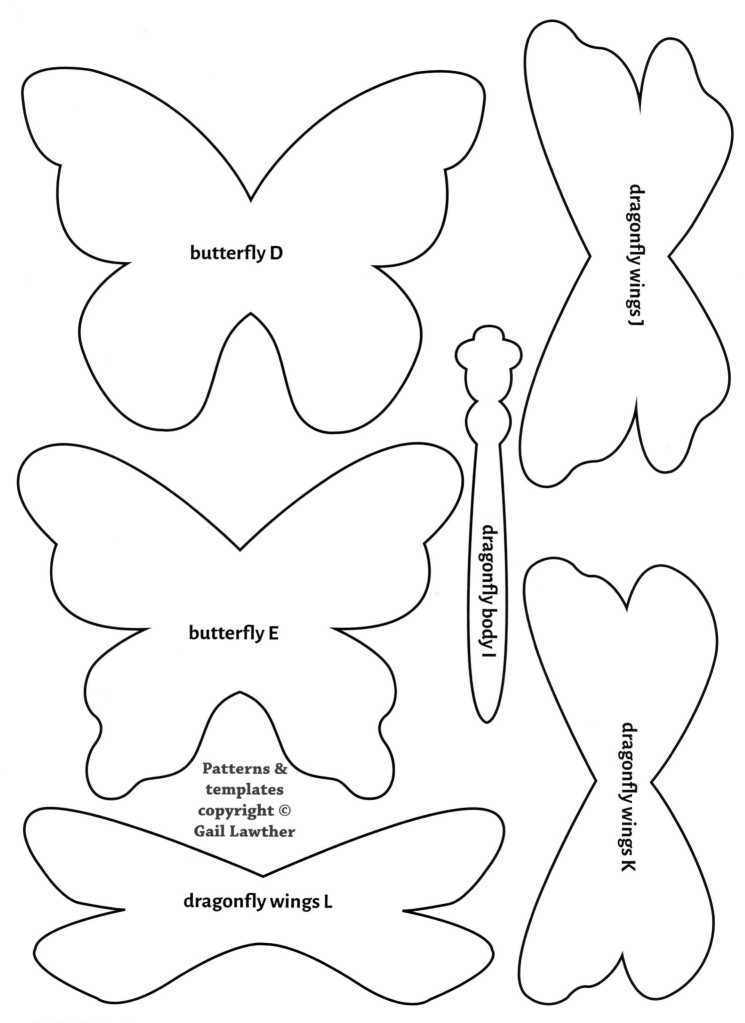

**butterfly D**

dragonfly wings J

dragonfly body I

**butterfly E**

Patterns &
templates
copyright ©
Gail Lawther

dragonfly wings K

**dragonfly wings L**

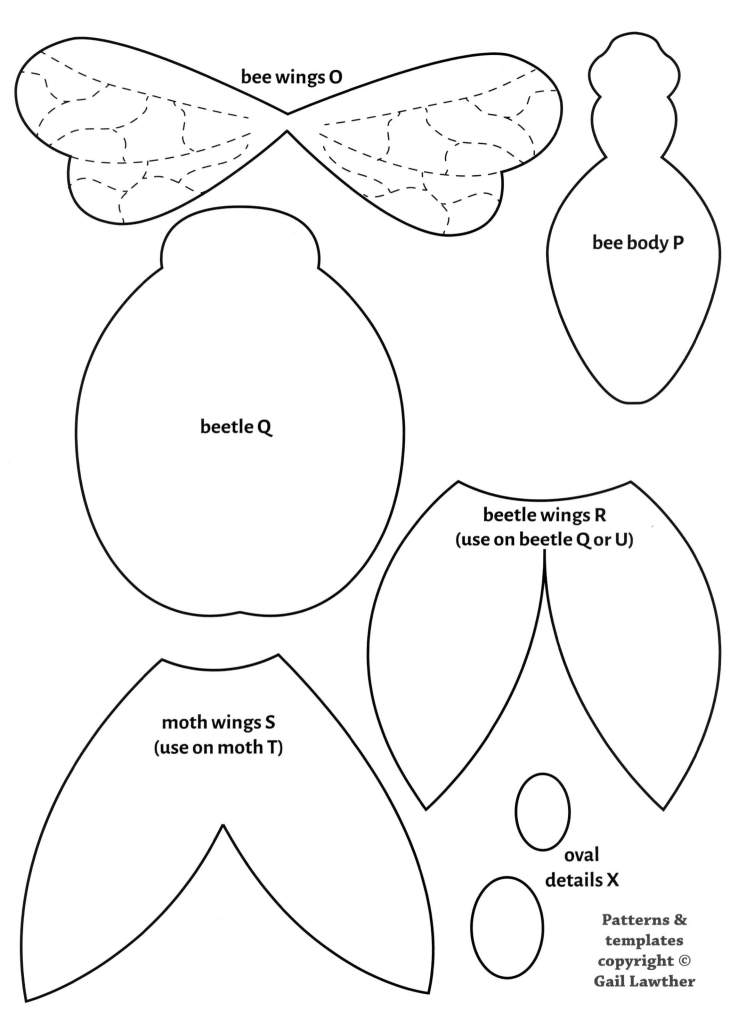

bee wings O

bee body P

beetle Q

beetle wings R
(use on beetle Q or U)

moth wings S
(use on moth T)

oval
details X

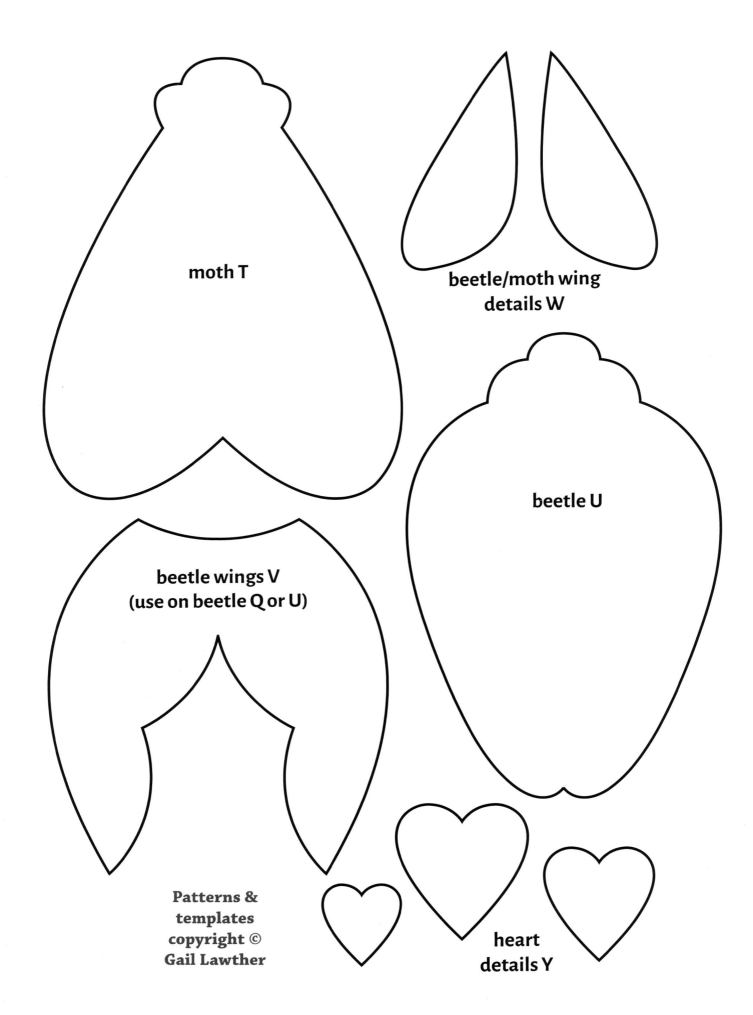

moth T

beetle/moth wing
details W

beetle U

beetle wings V
(use on beetle Q or U)

Patterns &
templates
copyright ©
Gail Lawther

heart
details Y